To:_____

*May these thoughts increase your desire
to know God better as you become aware
of his angels around you.*

From: _____

Angels aren't merely heavenly mailmen, carrying love letters, special offers, and dunning notices from heaven to earth. Their role has much greater dignity. More like ambassadors than message boys, they represent the very presence and intentions of God himself.

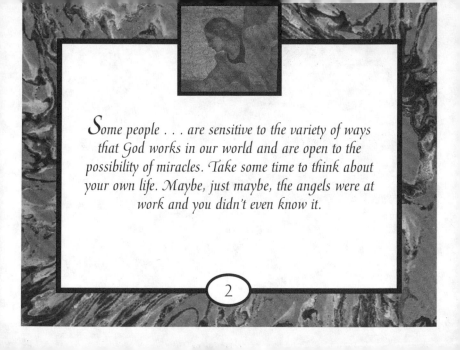

*S*ome people . . . are sensitive to the variety of ways that God works in our world and are open to the possibility of miracles. Take some time to think about your own life. Maybe, just maybe, the angels were at work and you didn't even know it.

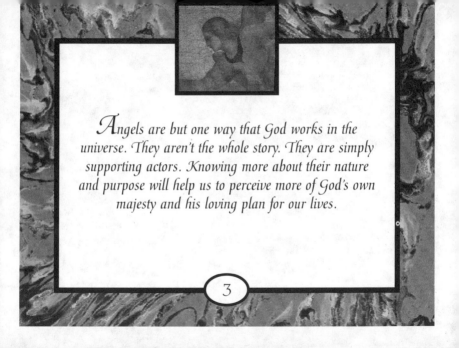

*A*ngels are but one way that God works in the universe. They aren't the whole story. They are simply supporting actors. Knowing more about their nature and purpose will help us to perceive more of God's own majesty and his loving plan for our lives.

*P*erhaps you are feeling thwarted in some way.
Ask humbly for God to guide you, and he will show
you if one of his angels is blocking the path ahead.
If he is, you dare not risk going forward.

4

*T*he Bible tells us that ... underneath are the everlasting arms of a mighty God. Whether my peril is physical, spiritual, or emotional, I know that God's strong arms and the arms of the mighty angels are there to hold me up when I am too weak to stand.

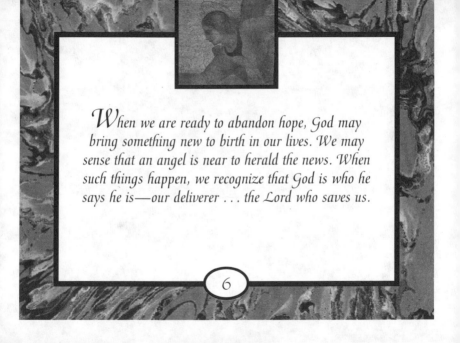

*W*hen we are ready to abandon hope, God may bring something new to birth in our lives. We may sense that an angel is near to herald the news. When such things happen, we recognize that God is who he says he is—our deliverer . . . the *L*ord who saves us.

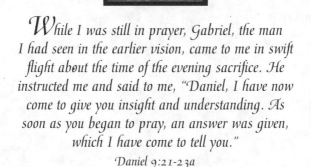

While I was still in prayer, Gabriel, the man I had seen in the earlier vision, came to me in swift flight about the time of the evening sacrifice. He instructed me and said to me, "Daniel, I have now come to give you insight and understanding. As soon as you began to pray, an answer was given, which I have come to tell you."

Daniel 9:21-23a

7

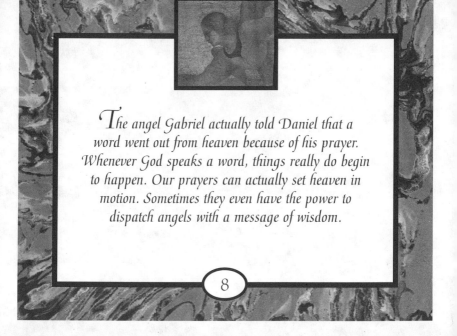

The angel Gabriel actually told Daniel that a word went out from heaven because of his prayer. Whenever God speaks a word, things really do begin to happen. Our prayers can actually set heaven in motion. Sometimes they even have the power to dispatch angels with a message of wisdom.

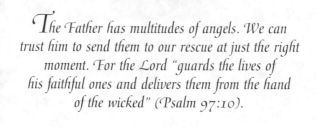

The Father has multitudes of angels. We can trust him to send them to our rescue at just the right moment. For the Lord "guards the lives of his faithful ones and delivers them from the hand of the wicked" (Psalm 97:10).

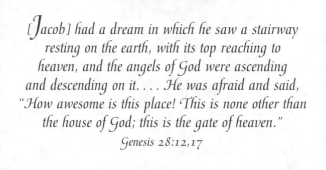

[Jacob] had a dream in which he saw a stairway resting on the earth, with its top reaching to heaven, and the angels of God were ascending and descending on it. . . . He was afraid and said, "How awesome is this place! This is none other than the house of God; this is the gate of heaven."

Genesis 28:12,17

$\mathcal{T}$he ladder in Jacob's dream symbolized the connection that exists between heaven and earth. The angels move up and down the ladder, bearing our needs to God and carrying his provision to us.

11

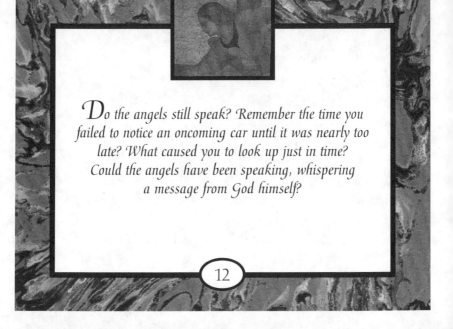

*D*o the angels still speak? Remember the time you failed to notice an oncoming car until it was nearly too late? What caused you to look up just in time? Could the angels have been speaking, whispering a message from God himself?

12

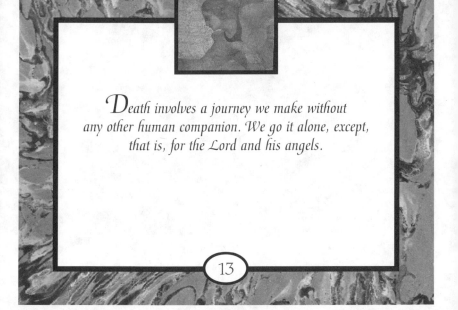

*D*eath involves a journey we make without
any other human companion. We go it alone, except,
that is, for the *L*ord and his angels.

One of the roles that angels play is to act as a kind of heavenly rescue squad. They often protect us from harm, both spiritual and physical. Sometimes these angelic rescues are obvious, but often they are not.

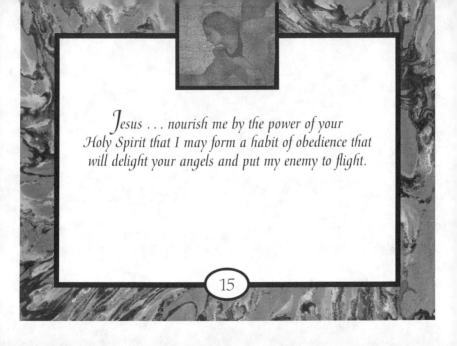

Jesus . . . nourish me by the power of your Holy Spirit that I may form a habit of obedience that will delight your angels and put my enemy to flight.

15

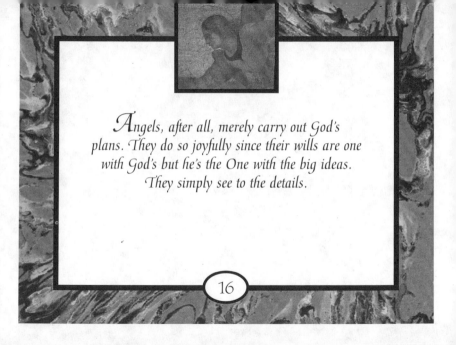

*A*ngels, after all, merely carry out God's plans. They do so joyfully since their wills are one with God's but he's the One with the big ideas. They simply see to the details.

16

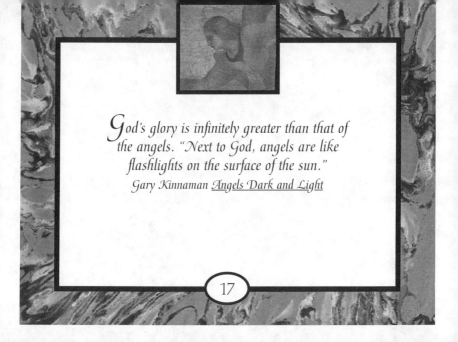

God's glory is infinitely greater than that of the angels. "Next to God, angels are like flashlights on the surface of the sun."

Gary Kinnaman Angels Dark and Light

*T*he angels show us that worship involves proclaiming the truth about God. When we are tempted to believe that God is other than holy—that he treats us . . . unkindly or unfaithfully, let us remember the truth of the angels' song.

*W*ith all this talk of angels, why isn't life more pleasant? Life is often painful ... because human beings have ... turned their hearts from God. Bad as this is ... we need to realize that not all the angels are on our side. "The devil is also near and about us."

Martin Luther

The angel of the LORD encamps around those
who fear him, and he delivers them.

Psalm 34:7

20

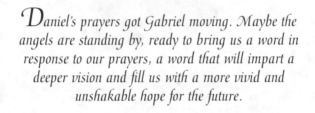

*D*aniel's prayers got Gabriel moving. Maybe the
angels are standing by, ready to bring us a word in
response to our prayers, a word that will impart a
deeper vision and fill us with a more vivid and
unshakable hope for the future.

21

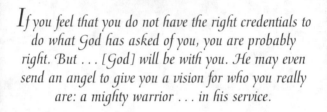

*I*f you feel that you do not have the right credentials to do what God has asked of you, you are probably right. But . . . [God] will be with you. He may even send an angel to give you a vision for who you really are: a mighty warrior . . . in his service.

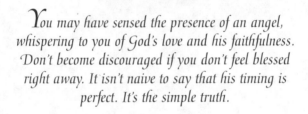

You may have sensed the presence of an angel, whispering to you of God's love and his faithfulness. Don't become discouraged if you don't feel blessed right away. It isn't naive to say that his timing is perfect. It's the simple truth.

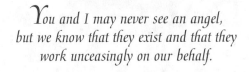

You and I may never see an angel, but we know that they exist and that they work unceasingly on our behalf.

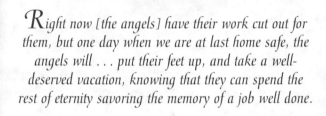

*R*ight now [the angels] have their work cut out for them, but one day when we are at last home safe, the angels will . . . put their feet up, and take a well-deserved vacation, knowing that they can spend the rest of eternity savoring the memory of a job well done.

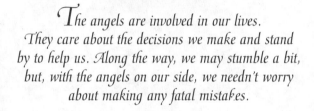

*T*he angels are involved in our lives.
They care about the decisions we make and stand
by to help us. Along the way, we may stumble a bit,
but, with the angels on our side, we needn't worry
about making any fatal mistakes.

26

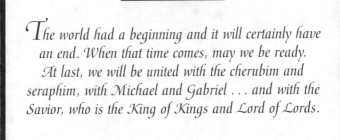

The world had a beginning and it will certainly have an end. When that time comes, may we be ready. At last, we will be united with the cherubim and seraphim, with Michael and Gabriel . . . and with the Savior, who is the King of Kings and Lord of Lords.

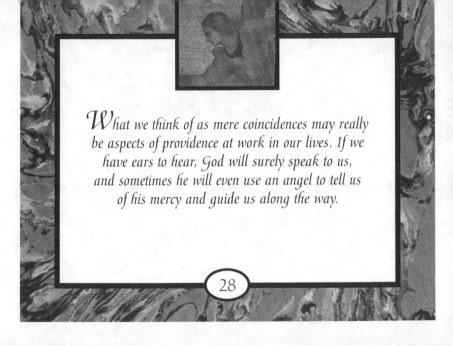

What we think of as mere coincidences may really be aspects of providence at work in our lives. If we have ears to hear, God will surely speak to us, and sometimes he will even use an angel to tell us of his mercy and guide us along the way.

28

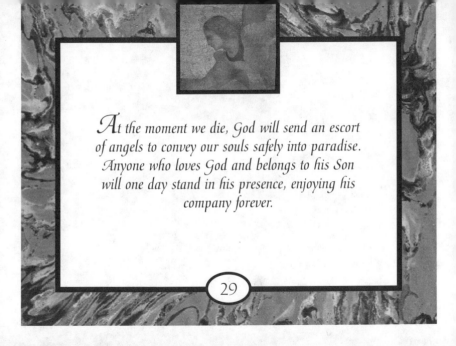

*A*t the moment we die, God will send an escort of angels to convey our souls safely into paradise. Anyone who loves God and belongs to his Son will one day stand in his presence, enjoying his company forever.

29

*S*ee that you do not look down on one of these
little ones. For I tell you that their angels in heaven
always see the face of my Father in heaven.

Matthew 18:10

30

*I*f you fear death, you can take tremendous comfort
that you and those you love will not have to make the
journey alone. [God] will surround you with his angels
to keep you from harm and lead you safely home.

The angels show us that it is not possible to refrain from worshipping God once you have given yourself to him and really beheld his face. Unlike us, their worship is not hindered by a veil separating them from the One they love.

*W*e may think that no one sees us when we act
in private, but in reality, we live in the presence
of God and the host of heaven.

*W*hether God is at work through his angels, directly through his Holy Spirit, or through us, doesn't really matter. What matters is that God loves us and finds an infinite number of ways to reassure us of that love.

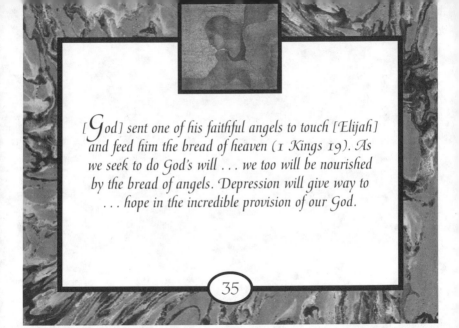

[God] sent one of his faithful angels to touch [Elijah] and feed him the bread of heaven (1 Kings 19). As we seek to do God's will ... we too will be nourished by the bread of angels. Depression will give way to ... hope in the incredible provision of our God.

35

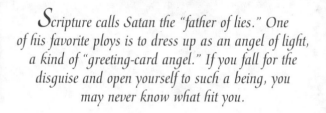

*S*cripture calls Satan the "father of lies." One of his favorite ploys is to dress up as an angel of light, a kind of "greeting-card angel." If you fall for the disguise and open yourself to such a being, you may never know what hit you.

*L*et us repeat and believe with the angels that God is full of might and that his arm is not too short to draw us out of our self-created darkness and into the light of his presence.

37

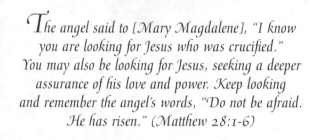

The angel said to [Mary Magdalene], "I know you are looking for Jesus who was crucified." You may also be looking for Jesus, seeking a deeper assurance of his love and power. Keep looking and remember the angel's words, "Do not be afraid. He has risen." (Matthew 28:1-6)

38

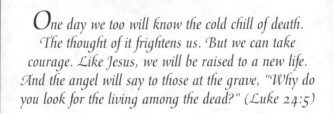

*O*ne day we too will know the cold chill of death. The thought of it frightens us. But we can take courage. Like Jesus, we will be raised to a new life. And the angel will say to those at the grave, "Why do you look for the living among the dead?" (Luke 24:5)

*F*or our struggle is not against flesh and blood, but against the rulers, against the authorities, against the powers of this dark world and against the spiritual forces of evil in the heavenly realms.

Ephesians 6:12

*I*t's just as well that God is the only one who has the power to order the angels around. He knows when and where they can do the most good.

41

If you find yourself in the wilderness [of the soul]. . . you may long for angels to whisper "courage" in your ears, but none come. In this kind of desert, remember to cling to God. With patience and faith you can emerge stronger and more hopeful than before.

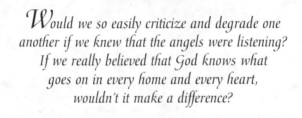

*W*ould we so easily criticize and degrade one
another if we knew that the angels were listening?
If we really believed that God knows what
goes on in every home and every heart,
wouldn't it make a difference?

[Shadrach, Meshach, and Abednego] had no way
of knowing they would miraculously survive their fiery
ordeal. They couldn't be sure God would send an
angel, but they trusted him for the outcome . . .
and God sent a fireproof angel to protect them as
they walked freely in the furnace.

*W*e must test the spirits against the Word of God and not allow our spiritual hungers to confuse our judgment. If we do . . . far from being a sitting duck for the devil, we will have the wisdom to discern the spirits, no matter how ingeniously disguised.

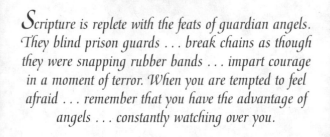

Scripture is replete with the feats of guardian angels. They blind prison guards ... break chains as though they were snapping rubber bands ... impart courage in a moment of terror. When you are tempted to feel afraid ... remember that you have the advantage of angels ... constantly watching over you.

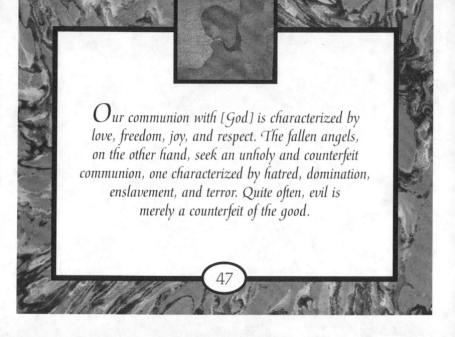

*O*ur communion with [God] is characterized by love, freedom, joy, and respect. The fallen angels, on the other hand, seek an unholy and counterfeit communion, one characterized by hatred, domination, enslavement, and terror. Quite often, evil is merely a counterfeit of the good.

*A*s God's people . . . our task is to continue to
pray for our enemies. If we do, we will be certain
to stand on the side of [God's] angels.

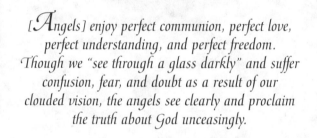

[Angels] enjoy perfect communion, perfect love,
perfect understanding, and perfect freedom.
Though we "see through a glass darkly" and suffer
confusion, fear, and doubt as a result of our
clouded vision, the angels see clearly and proclaim
the truth about God unceasingly.

*P*raise the LORD, you his angels, you mighty ones who do his bidding, who obey his word.

Psalm 103:20

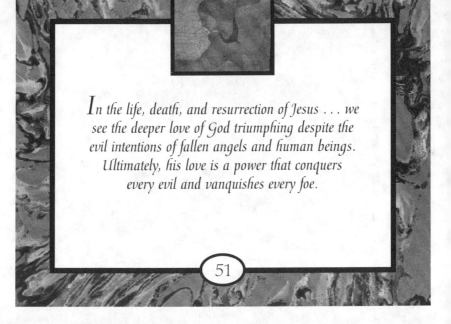

In the life, death, and resurrection of Jesus . . . we see the deeper love of God triumphing despite the evil intentions of fallen angels and human beings. Ultimately, his love is a power that conquers every evil and vanquishes every foe.

51

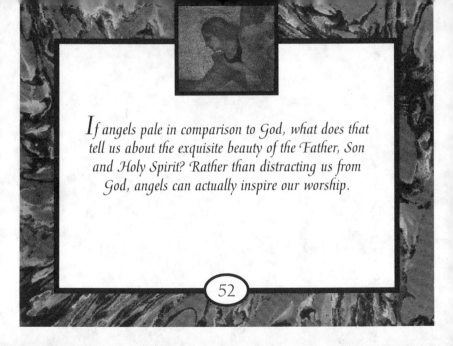

*I*f angels pale in comparison to God, what does that tell us about the exquisite beauty of the Father, Son and Holy Spirit? Rather than distracting us from God, angels can actually inspire our worship.

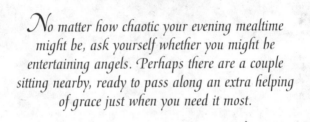

*N*o matter how chaotic your evening mealtime might be, ask yourself whether you might be entertaining angels. Perhaps there are a couple sitting nearby, ready to pass along an extra helping of grace just when you need it most.

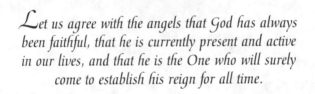

$\mathcal{L}$et us agree with the angels that God has always been faithful, that he is currently present and active in our lives, and that he is the One who will surely come to establish his reign for all time.

*A*ngels reflect the glory of God and are active
in our world only to do his bidding. If we let
them, angels can be a window to God, offering a
glimpse of his power, his goodness, and his
loving intentions toward us.

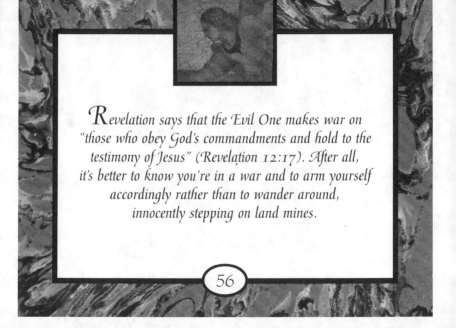

Revelation says that the Evil One makes war on "those who obey God's commandments and hold to the testimony of Jesus" (Revelation 12:17). After all, it's better to know you're in a war and to arm yourself accordingly rather than to wander around, innocently stepping on land mines.

*P*erhaps you have received a few messages from Satan: . . . a tongue-lashing from your boss, a crippling disease, a catastrophe that strikes your family. Plead to God to take your affliction away. But listen while you're in God's presence. He might have a deeper message than the one Satan intends to deliver.

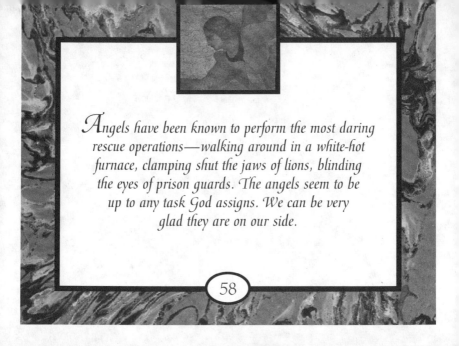

Angels have been known to perform the most daring rescue operations—walking around in a white-hot furnace, clamping shut the jaws of lions, blinding the eyes of prison guards. The angels seem to be up to any task God assigns. We can be very glad they are on our side.

It's important to realize that the good angels aren't always sweetness and light to everyone they meet. Scripture shows the angels ministering God's judgment nearly as frequently as they carry his messages.

59

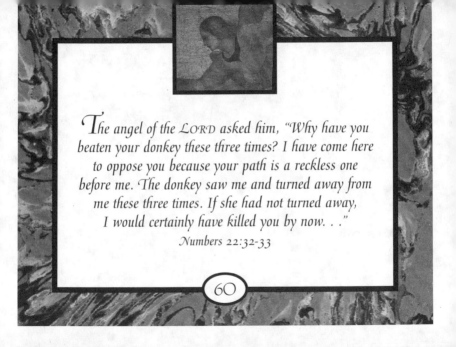

The angel of the LORD asked him, "Why have you beaten your donkey these three times? I have come here to oppose you because your path is a reckless one before me. The donkey saw me and turned away from me these three times. If she had not turned away, I would certainly have killed you by now. . ."

Numbers 22:32-33

60

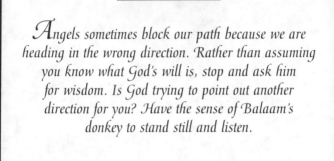

Angels sometimes block our path because we are heading in the wrong direction. Rather than assuming you know what God's will is, stop and ask him for wisdom. Is God trying to point out another direction for you? Have the sense of Balaam's donkey to stand still and listen.

61

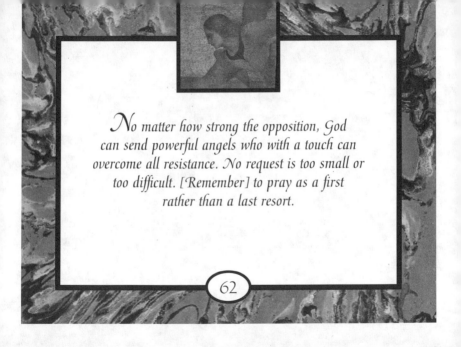

*N*o matter how strong the opposition, God can send powerful angels who with a touch can overcome all resistance. *N*o request is too small or too difficult. [Remember] to pray as a first rather than a last resort.

62

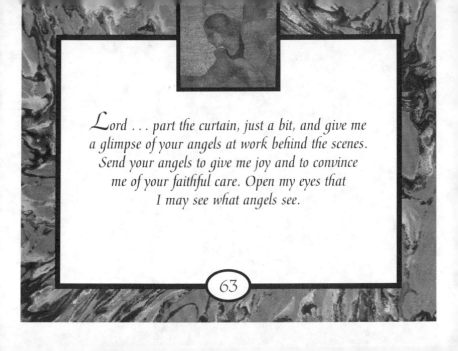

*Lord . . . part the curtain, just a bit, and give me
a glimpse of your angels at work behind the scenes.
Send your angels to give me joy and to convince
me of your faithful care. Open my eyes that
I may see what angels see.*

63

*T*he seraphim are some of the more exotic angels described in the Bible. They live constantly in the presence of God, surrounding and guarding his throne and singing his praises. They are called "the burning ones," perhaps because they reflect God's holiness.

When the angel of the LORD appeared to Gideon, he said, "The LORD is with you, mighty warrior." ... The LORD turned to him and said, "Go in the strength you have and save Israel out of Midian's hand. Am I not sending you?" ... Gideon asked, "How can I save Israel? My clan is the weakest in Manasseh, and I am the least in my family."

Judges 6:12,14-15

*G*ideon was a farmer . . . and yet the angel called him a mighty warrior . . . and commissioned Gideon to save Israel from their enemies. The angel knew what he was talking about. The reason Gideon succeeded was not because of who he was, but because the Lord was with him.

66

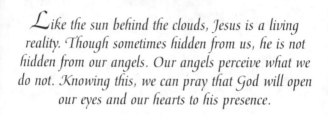

*L*ike the sun behind the clouds, Jesus is a living reality. Though sometimes hidden from us, he is not hidden from our angels. Our angels perceive what we do not. Knowing this, we can pray that God will open our eyes and our hearts to his presence.

*H*agar was a single mother who was homeless, jobless, and penniless. Suddenly, in the midst of nowhere, an angel spoke to her from heaven. The strong and comforting words of the angel dispelled her fear. A strange, new peace came with the angel's message. God would provide.

*W*e will often suffer loss, fear, confusion, and pain in our quest to be faithful to what and whom we believe in. As we trust God for the outcome . . . perhaps an angel will even stand by our side . . . protecting us from the devouring flames that threaten to consume us.

69

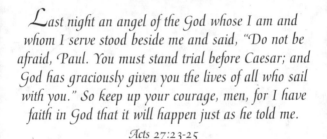

Last night an angel of the God whose I am and whom I serve stood beside me and said, "Do not be afraid, Paul. You must stand trial before Caesar; and God has graciously given you the lives of all who sail with you." So keep up your courage, men, for I have faith in God that it will happen just as he told me.

Acts 27:23-25

Paul had been terrified by the storm. The angel
calmed his fears and ... imparted new courage
to Paul. In turn, Paul was able to encourage others.
Like Paul we can find courage in the word that
God speaks to us and ... we can, in turn,
encourage those around us.

71

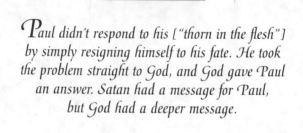

*P*aul didn't respond to his ["thorn in the flesh"]
by simply resigning himself to his fate. He took
the problem straight to God, and God gave Paul
an answer. Satan had a message for Paul,
but God had a deeper message.

*A*ngels continually enjoy . . . face-to-face
communion with God. They are not seduced,
as we are, into making idols out of lesser desires.
Why would you choose fool's gold when you
know where the mother lode is?

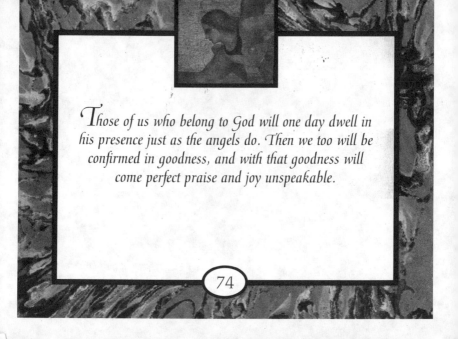

Those of us who belong to God will one day dwell in his presence just as the angels do. Then we too will be confirmed in goodness, and with that goodness will come perfect praise and joy unspeakable.

Jesus went out as usual to the Mount of Olives, and his disciples followed him. He withdrew about a stone's throw beyond them, knelt down and prayed, "Father, if you are willing, take this cup from me; yet not my will, but yours be done." An angel from heaven appeared to him and strengthened him.

Luke 22:39,41-43

75

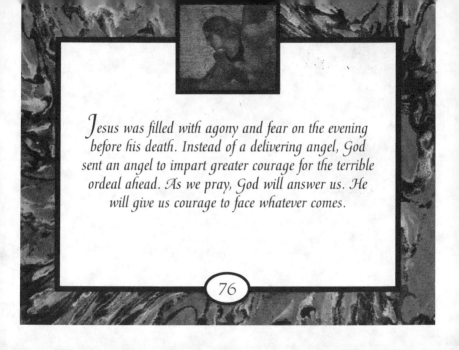

Jesus was filled with agony and fear on the evening before his death. Instead of a delivering angel, God sent an angel to impart greater courage for the terrible ordeal ahead. As we pray, God will answer us. He will give us courage to face whatever comes.

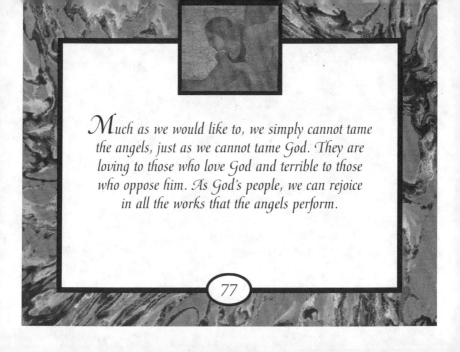

$\mathcal{M}$uch as we would like to, we simply cannot tame the angels, just as we cannot tame God. They are loving to those who love God and terrible to those who oppose him. As God's people, we can rejoice in all the works that the angels perform.

77

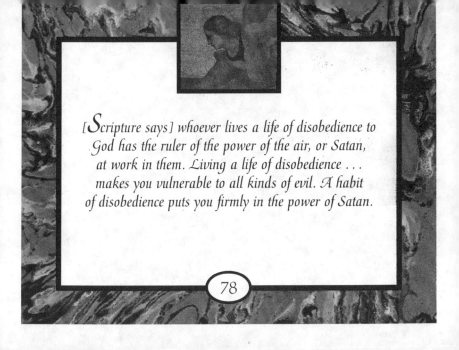

[*S*cripture says] whoever lives a life of disobedience to God has the ruler of the power of the air, or Satan, at work in them. Living a life of disobedience ... makes you vulnerable to all kinds of evil. A habit of disobedience puts you firmly in the power of Satan.

Though the God of the universe beckons, calling us into his holy presence, we are often . . . too busy for him. The angels must be scandalized. They know that God has invited us to share a wonderful intimacy with him, but wonder how we could possibly take that privilege for granted.

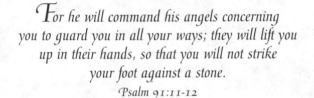

*F*or he will command his angels concerning
you to guard you in all your ways; they will lift you
up in their hands, so that you will not strike
your foot against a stone.

Psalm 91:11-12

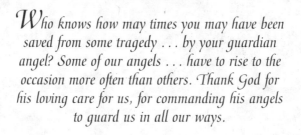

Who knows how may times you may have been saved from some tragedy . . . by your guardian angel? Some of our angels . . . have to rise to the occasion more often than others. Thank God for his loving care for us, for commanding his angels to guard us in all our ways.

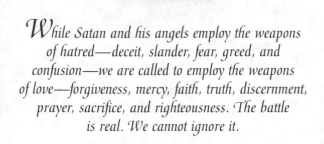

*W*hile Satan and his angels employ the weapons
of hatred—deceit, slander, fear, greed, and
confusion—we are called to employ the weapons
of love—forgiveness, mercy, faith, truth, discernment,
prayer, sacrifice, and righteousness. The battle
is real. We cannot ignore it.

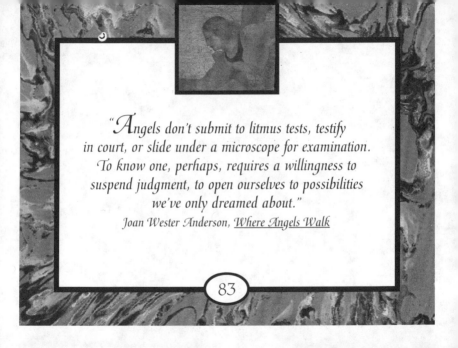

"*Angels don't submit to litmus tests, testify in court, or slide under a microscope for examination. To know one, perhaps, requires a willingness to suspend judgment, to open ourselves to possibilities we've only dreamed about.*"

Joan Wester Anderson, *Where Angels Walk*

83

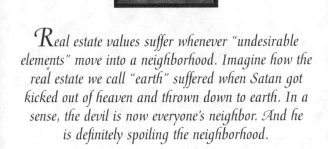

*R*eal estate values suffer whenever "undesirable elements" move into a neighborhood. Imagine how the real estate we call "earth" suffered when Satan got kicked out of heaven and thrown down to earth. In a sense, the devil is now everyone's neighbor. And he is definitely spoiling the neighborhood.

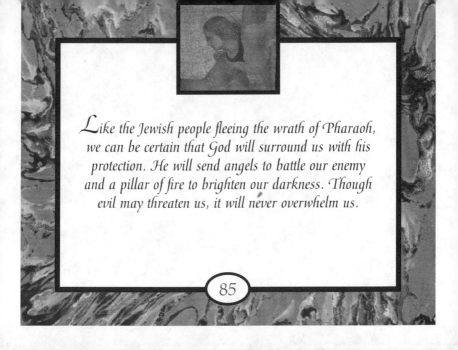

$\mathcal{L}$ike the Jewish people fleeing the wrath of Pharaoh, we can be certain that God will surround us with his protection. He will send angels to battle our enemy and a pillar of fire to brighten our darkness. Though evil may threaten us, it will never overwhelm us.

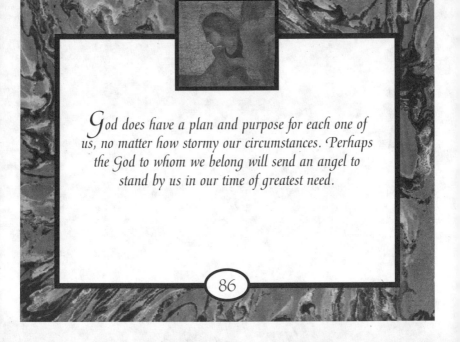

God does have a plan and purpose for each one of us, no matter how stormy our circumstances. Perhaps the God to whom we belong will send an angel to stand by us in our time of greatest need.

*W*hen the world becomes blind and deaf to God, he resorts to drastic measures. To catch our attention, the angels sound the harsh notes of the trumpet (Revelation 8:6-7) . . . sounding the large notes of God's mercy so that human beings will admit their desperate need and be reconciled to God .

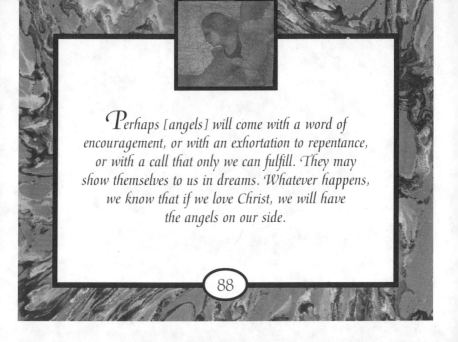

Perhaps [angels] will come with a word of encouragement, or with an exhortation to repentance, or with a call that only we can fulfill. They may show themselves to us in dreams. Whatever happens, we know that if we love Christ, we will have the angels on our side.

88

$\mathcal{M}$uch like aerobic exercise that increases lung capacity, preferring God's will to your own can increase your spiritual stamina. You will be stronger and more joyful, better able to resist the enticements of the evil angels, no matter how appealing they may seem.

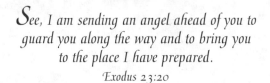

*S*ee, I am sending an angel ahead of you to
guard you along the way and to bring you
to the place I have prepared.

Exodus 23:20

We don't know the challenges we will face tomorrow morning let alone next year or the year after. But God does, and he can set his angels in motion on our behalf!

*M*ichael the *A*rchangel is depicted in Scripture as
a great warrior, leading the host of heaven against . . .
the demons of hell. He is also thought to be the
guardian protector of God's people. It is comforting
to know that powerful angels like Michael are
engaged in the battle alongside us.

*W*hy do some people see angels while others see nothing? Perhaps some of us have the kind of simple faith that invites the angels to show up.

93

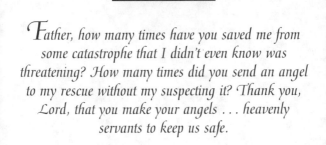

Father, how many times have you saved me from some catastrophe that I didn't even know was threatening? How many times did you send an angel to my rescue without my suspecting it? Thank you, Lord, that you make your angels ... heavenly servants to keep us safe.

*W*hen the Son of Man comes in his glory,
and all the angels with him, he will sit on his
throne in heavenly glory.

Matthew 25:31

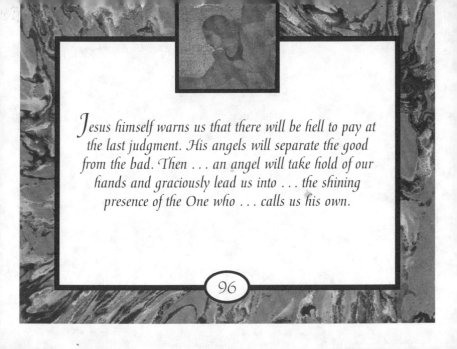

*J*esus himself warns us that there will be hell to pay at the last judgment. His angels will separate the good from the bad. Then . . . an angel will take hold of our hands and graciously lead us into . . . the shining presence of the One who . . . calls us his own.

*W*e will surely face pressure to compromise our beliefs in order to fit in with the world around us. When that happens ... remember that you can sell your soul by making the wrong kind of compromises. Remember that God protects the blameless person. And last of all, remember the angels.

*I*f God hadn't spoken to her through the angel,
Hagar and her son would have died of thirst a stone's
throw away from a well brimming with water.
Perhaps God will send an angel to show you just how
close his provision is for you.

98

Augustine says that "one loving soul sets another on fire." Perhaps that's what the angels can do for us. Try learning from the seraphim ... burning with love as you behold God's beauty, his power, and his loving-kindness.

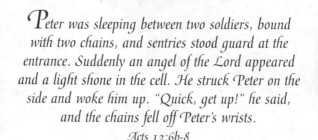

*P*eter was sleeping between two soldiers, bound
with two chains, and sentries stood guard at the
entrance. Suddenly an angel of the *L*ord appeared
and a light shone in the cell. *H*e struck Peter on the
side and woke him up. "*Q*uick, get up!" he said,
and the chains fell off Peter's wrists.

Acts 12:6b-8

*A*ngels possess far greater power than the powers of evil that threaten us. It took only one guardian angel to hoodwink four squads of soldiers who were standing guard. The chains literally fell off Peter's wrists, and he walked out of prison and into the city a free man.

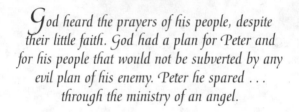

God heard the prayers of his people, despite
their little faith. *God* had a plan for Peter and
for his people that would not be subverted by any
evil plan of his enemy. Peter he spared . . .
through the ministry of an angel.

*W*hy do some people see angels while others see nothing? Perhaps the answer lies with both God and us. The Lord has reasons we may never understand for opening the eyes of one person and shutting the eyes of another.

103

The angels have played a part in our past and in our present, and they will certainly play an important role in our future. How can we go wrong when the angels are rooting for us?

All-consuming love is a gift that comes only from the hand of God. Why not ask God for this gift so that you can compete with the angels in your passion for God? You may not surpass them, but what joy you will discover in trying!

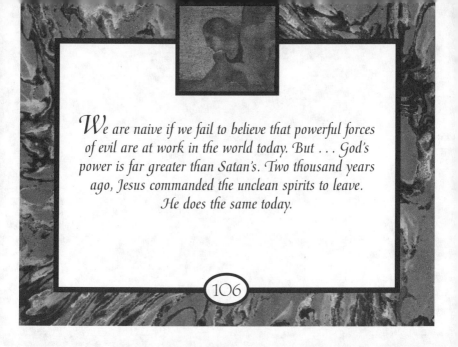

We are naive if we fail to believe that powerful forces
of evil are at work in the world today. But . . . God's
power is far greater than Satan's. Two thousand years
ago, Jesus commanded the unclean spirits to leave.
He does the same today.

106

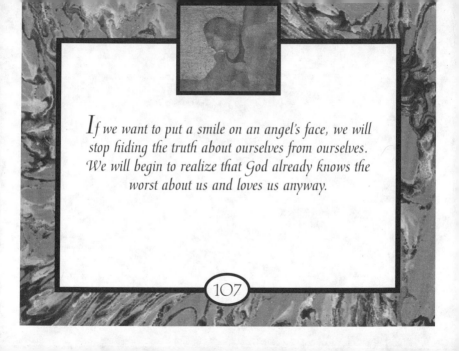

*I*f we want to put a smile on an angel's face, we will stop hiding the truth about ourselves from ourselves. We will begin to realize that God already knows the worst about us and loves us anyway.

107

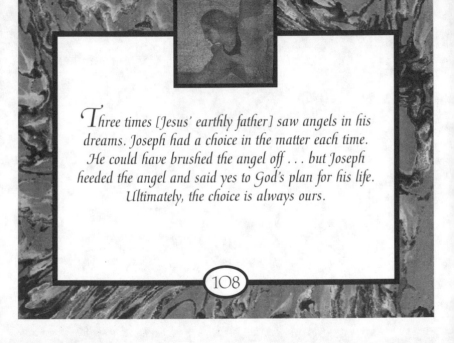

Three times [Jesus' earthly father] saw angels in his
dreams. Joseph had a choice in the matter each time.
He could have brushed the angel off . . . but Joseph
heeded the angel and said yes to God's plan for his life.
Ultimately, the choice is always ours.

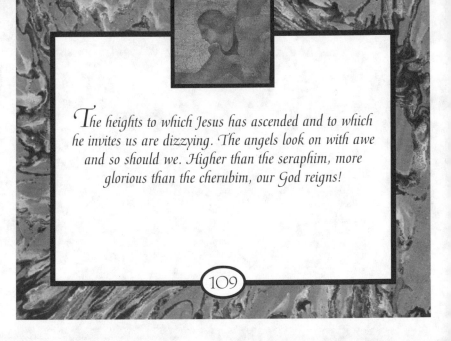

The heights to which Jesus has ascended and to which he invites us are dizzying. The angels look on with awe and so should we. Higher than the seraphim, more glorious than the cherubim, our God reigns!

There were shepherds living out in the fields nearby, keeping watch over their flocks at night. An angel of the Lord appeared to them, and the glory of the Lord shone around them, and they were terrified.

Luke 2:8-9

110

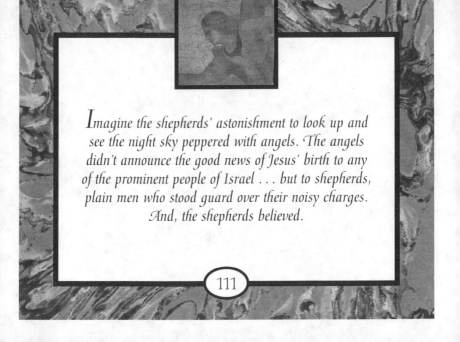

*Imagine the shepherds' astonishment to look up and
see the night sky peppered with angels. The angels
didn't announce the good news of Jesus' birth to any
of the prominent people of Israel . . . but to shepherds,
plain men who stood guard over their noisy charges.
And, the shepherds believed.*

111

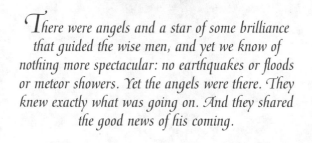

There were angels and a star of some brilliance
that guided the wise men, and yet we know of
nothing more spectacular: no earthquakes or floods
or meteor showers. Yet the angels were there. They
knew exactly what was going on. And they shared
the good news of his coming.

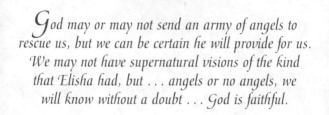

*G*od may or may not send an army of angels to rescue us, but we can be certain he will provide for us. We may not have supernatural visions of the kind that Elisha had, but ... angels or no angels, we will know without a doubt ... God is faithful.

One of the roles angels play in human affairs is to convey messages between God and human beings. Unfortunately, it seems that Satan likes to send messages of his own from time to time. Remember who the "author of confusion" really is.

114

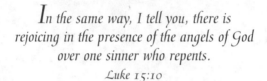

*In the same way, I tell you, there is
rejoicing in the presence of the angels of God
over one sinner who repents.*

Luke 15:10

*B*ecause the angels love us, they want to see us reconciled to the source of all joy, to *G*od himself. The angels themselves are rejoicing over us, the one sinner who repents.

116

$\mathcal{D}$arius had rolled a stone over the lions' den. Yet an angel had pressed the lions' jaws shut and saved Daniel's life. Religious authorities in Jerusalem would place a similar stone over the tomb of Jesus. Once again, mere stones could not stop God's angels. Remember Daniel . . . Jesus . . . the angels. Be faithful.

*W*hat is it with angels and birth announcements?
[In Scripture] the angel Gabriel announced . . .
the coming birth of a special child. The circumstances
were next to impossible. God seemed to be making
a point through these surprise announcements.
What was impossible for men and women
was a simple matter for God.

The guards posted at [Jesus'] tomb were terrified when they saw the angel. Scripture says they "became like dead men." Dealing with the guards must have been like flicking ants off a picnic plate. No power on earth could suppress the good news that the angel had come to announce.

119

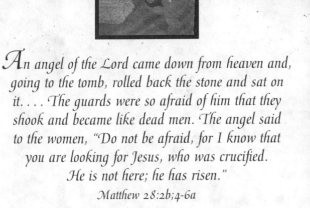

An angel of the Lord came down from heaven and, going to the tomb, rolled back the stone and sat on it. . . . The guards were so afraid of him that they shook and became like dead men. The angel said to the women, "Do not be afraid, for I know that you are looking for Jesus, who was crucified. He is not here; he has risen."

Matthew 28:2b;4-6a

120

Requests for information should be addressed to:
  Zondervan Publishing House
  5300 Patterson Avenue, S.E.
  Grand Rapids, Michigan 49530

Project Editor: Sarah Hupp
Design: Patricia L. Matthews
Photography: Superstock

Printed in the United States of America

95 96 97 /❖ CH/ 3 2 1